EVEN MORE

LESSONS LEARNED

FROM OUR

MISSTAKES

Michael Rosman

www.TheCorporateCaterer.com

DEDICATION

This book is dedicated to you, and my readership family. *Even More Lessons Learned from Our Mistakes* is the third volume in the "Lessons Learned" series. The response from the first volume, *Lessons Learned from Our Mistakes*, was so overwhelming, it led to a second volume, *More Lessons Learned from Our Mistakes*. Humbled again by the feedback, including a group chant, "We Want More! We Want More" at a conference I was speaking at, "Even More" seemed like the next logical step.

It is perhaps beyond my writing abilities to adequately express the gratitude I feel every time I receive an email, or phone call, or meet someone in person who says, "I read your book, and it's been very helpful..."

To all of you, my comrades in this crazy business we're in, Thank you so much. As you read thru these pages, as I often say, "Let my pain be your gain."

Enjoy!

-Michael

PREFACE

Demand for corporate drop-off catering is booming. Industry analysts report this segment now accounts for one-third of a twelve billion-dollar-a-year industry. And the future shines bright, as experts predict consumer demand for "food delivered to businesses" will grow steadily over the next decade, as it is still an under-tapped market.

If you operate a commercial kitchen and are watching this money train pass you by, it's time to get on board! If you want to fast-track your growth, consider The Corporate Caterer as your co-pilot on the journey.

We offer an array of services for all levels of experience. Whether you are just starting out and don't know where to begin, or have an existing client base and want to take your business to the next level, or a (multi) million-dollar a year operation and want to conquer even more of the market share, we have built The Roadmap for you.

THE GATEWAY

Please visit TheCorporateCaterer.com for information about our membership services. Our multimedia website shares behind-the-scenes tips, customizable templates and menus, checklists and worksheets, sample sales scripts, videos, recorded conferences, and how-to resources for operating a financially successful corporate drop-off/delivery catering business.

Additionally, we offer customized:

- Virtual Coaching Membership Packages
- Catering Leads Membership Packages
- Lead Generation Program
- On-Site Consulting Services
- Menu Creation and Updating Services
- Playbook for Your Operation

If you would like to speak to Michael directly or schedule a complimentary consultation to discuss your businesses goals, please call our corporate office at 781-641-3303.

ACKNOWLEDGMENT

Richard Radbil is a colleague who owned and operated a very successful corporate catering business in Wisconsin for 30 years. Today, he is happily retired from the industry. However, like most of us, the food business remains in his blood.

In addition to Richard being a valued partner of our consulting team, he has graciously collaborated on some of the content in these pages.

INTRODUCTION

Even More Lessons Learned from Our Mistakes, is the continuation in the "Lessons Learned" series.

It offers a new a new compilation of "reality catering" missteps, screw-ups, ill-conceived game plans, wrong decisions (that felt right at the time), and the lessons learned over thirty years in the restaurant and catering industry.

In addition, *Even More Lessons Learned from Our Mistakes*, offers concrete information and suggestions to help your company not merely survive - but thrive.

As I advise my members and clients, think of your business as a continuous work in progress. (As I do, with The Corporate Caterer). There is no finish line. Our "to-do" list will never be complete. Commit to doing one thing, every day, that will make your operation a tick better. Because those ticks add up.

BUT ARE YOU MAKING MONEY?

As a corporate catering consultant, I inevitably develop an emotional investment in my client's success. Business aside, when I see their catering operation become more efficient and profitable in connection with the work we have done together, it nourishes me.

Whether I am engaging in one-to-one coaching, or on-site consulting, the first question I ask is the same.

"IS YOUR OPERATION?

a) Making Money?

b) Breaking-Even?

c) Losing Money?

d) You're Not Sure?"

In 2016, we asked this question to 487 of our website members at www.TheCorporateCaterer.com

The Results?

a) 190 - Making Money (39%)

c)   97 - Breaking-Even (20%)

b)   93 - Losing Money (19%)

d) 107 - Not Sure (22%)

"Making Money"

"Are you paying yourself a salary?" is my follow up question to this response. If you're not, your P/L is incomplete. Your salary is part of the equation. It would be the equivalent of saying; "My labor cost is only 20% - when I don't include my head chef's salary."

This begs the question, "How much should I pay myself?" The answer is, "Whatever you would have to pay someone qualified to do your job." After you have paid all your bills, any cash in the bank at the end of your fiscal year is profit.

"Breaking Even"

Breaking even means paying yourself and all current bills. At the end of the year, your bottom-line profit and loss statement is zero. Your business, in essence, has created you a job.

"Losing Money"

I try to be direct and to the point. That said, I believe a lot of us in this business are a tick crazy, (myself included) - but we wear it as a badge of honor. Why else would we voluntarily work in an industry that is notorious for being long on hours and short on profit?

Is there a piece of our DNA that makes us gluttons for punishment?

My theory is that we are all privileged victims of this business being in our blood. Despite the often-grueling workload, the unpredictable schedule, the holidays spent working at the cost of family time and the "far from laughing all-the-way to the bank" reality, most days, we love what we do.

In fact, I challenge any other industry to prove their workforce possesses the same level passion for their craft.

Is there a single owner or operator of a catering company, restaurant, franchise, food-truck, corporate dining facility or private chef, who is not in business to make money? Making an assumption the answer is, "No," why did only 39% of respondents from my survey report showing a profit?

It is usually a combination of factors, including:

• Not keeping a close enough eye on the books.

•Not having an efficient a system for tracking sales and expenses.

• Feeling overwhelmed by the day-to-day pressures of successfully getting orders out the door, while putting out the fire du-jour.

• Have not embraced the concept that every single paid order must yield an acceptable profit margin. Period. It is not your job to provide clients with food and services that they are not budgeted for. All this does is chip away from your bottom line.

It is your job to provide clients with proposals and menu options that fit their budgets while staying true to your prices.

I recently had a client excitedly tell me, "For the first time, we broke the million dollar mark!" 'That's terrific," I replied. "How much money went out the door to reach that million?" As her face scrunched-up, she paused, and said, "I'm not sure." "Figure it out and let me know," I requested.

She came to my office three days later and looked like she'd been hit by a Mack truck. Or perhaps had drank a bottle of vodka the night before. Or possibly, both.

"Are you ok Maycie?" I asked, "You don't look so hot." "No, I'm not. I have an answer to your question. It cost us $1.1 million to generate $1 million in revenue "

Ouch.

I would much prefer to have a client say, "We did $100,000 in sales, and our expenses, (including an owners salary), were $90,000." This is a better-run operation. I have seen too many owners seduced by their sales figures.

If your core business model is not set-up properly, or you have veered off course, doing more business (even ten times more), than the other guy doesn't always mean you are making more money. In fact, it can mean the opposite.

If you are losing money, it's time to do something about it – now. If you keep pounding your head against the wall long enough, eventually it starts to hurt. If you do not make changes, one day your coffers will run dry. You will be out of business.

Maybe your labor or food costs are higher than they should be? Perhaps it's time to approach your landlord about a rent reduction based on market conditions?

Does your catering menu need price adjustments? (We never use the term "price increases"). It could be a combination, as well as other operational issues.

"You Are Not Sure"

First off, there is no shame in this answer. The only shame would be if, after reading this book, getting an answer, determining the financial heath of your business, does not shoot to the very top on your to-do list.

How much money is coming in vs. how much is going out? This is Business 101. Ironically, for all the hours so many of us work, too many operators do not pay close enough attention to the most important factors that determine your chances for success.

It reminds me of the adage that people spend more time planning a vacation than they do their retirement.

If you're not sure, it's time to dive into your books, bills, invoices, accounts payable and accounts receivable. To whatever degree you think your record keeping is a disaster, I guarantee you I have seen worse.

I tell my clients, "This is a judgment-free zone. I have walked in your shoes – and I have. The mission now is to move forward and right the ship. If you want help, it's available."

One day, you will decide it is time to sell your business. Showing profitable books will net you the maximum selling price.

Guidelines for a Profitable Corporate Drop-Off Business:

(Based on percentage of sales)

Note: These expenses can vary depending on your specific operation, the State you do business in, and your total number of employees.

<u>Food Cost</u>
30%-32%

<u>Rent / Mortgage</u>
8%-10%

<u>Labor</u> (Including paying yourself)
30%-31%

<u>Disposables</u> (Paper goods, plastic ware, serving trays, dome lids)
3%

Business Insurance/Workers Comp
3%

Utilities
5%

Advertising
2%

Maintenance / Repairs
3%

Vehicle Expenses
3%

Legal / Accounting
2%

Telephone / Internet
1%

Total Operating Expenses = 90% - 95%

Example:

• For a corporate catering business generating $1,000,000 in annual revenue.

 > Total operating expenses (including owners salary) should be $900,000 - $950,000

> Bottom-line profit should be $50,000 - $100,000

Carl Sacks, Vice-President of Business Development at Catersource, recently reported, "Some caterers have shown a pretax profit of over 25%, but the average pre-tax profit of all caterers we have worked with over the years has been 7% - 8%.

In painting a slightly broader brush, I align with a formula that results in a 5% – 10% profit range. These are tighter margins than other industries. This is why all aspects of your business need to be firing on all cylinders.

Gut Check

Goggling "why my business isn't making money" will result in plenty of reading material. A list of the usual suspects includes lack of working capital, sloppy record keeping, ineffective marketing, and poor decision-making.

These however, are all symptoms. They are not the specific problems.

While these symptoms can precipitate your catering business/restaurant struggles, or lack of profit, we must dig deeper. These are some of the bigger, more fundamental problems why you may be the proverbial rat running on the wheel.

1) Unrealistic Expectations

Whether your corporate drop-off division is in its infancy, or if you have a solid client base and want to take it to the next level, it is a process. There is no magic wand. It requires a current state-of-affairs analysis, making a plan and defining a step-by-step strategy. That is only the beginning. That is the easy part.

Implementing the plan is where the work begins. Staying fully committed to the plan, with no let-up – even when it feels like you are not getting anywhere, which is not uncommon the first couple of months, is where the real work is.

This is what separates the contenders from the pretenders.

The Corporate Caterer has a roadmap, a blueprint for success. Assuming a client and their staff are committed and follow-thru with the plan, six months is a good benchmark for when you will look up and say, "Ok, I get it. This is starting to all come together."

A key indicator of, "starting to all come together," is when you begin amassing *repeat business* – the golden goose of corporate catering.

2) Handling Setbacks

Setbacks are inevitable. More often then not, how the business owner and management team respond to these hurdles will shape the future success or failure of the company.

Even when a colossal event, such as the stock market crashing and the entire economy is knocked off its feet, or widely-reported bad publicity due to a health inspection or safety issue, (for example, Chipotles recent food-poising across the country), there is often much that can be learned, altered, and applied for the future.

3) Being dependent on a single large account

Our corporate division in Boston generates $2 million annually. Our largest account represents 7.5% of total business. We have committed to not having too many eggs in one basket.

If, or when, we lose a big account (and I say when, because it is almost inevitable). Either the company builds an in-house cafeteria because it makes sense financially, or after years of your food, change is made for the sake of change. (No one wants to eat at their favorite restaurant every night), the effects are not devastating.

It's the sports adage that head coaches are hired to one day be fired. When you land those monster accounts, savor them. Your services almost inevitably have a certain shelf life.

Much earlier in my career, I was in the opposite situation. We had one huge account that represented almost 50% of our business.

It was a great ride for three-and-a-half years. When they decided it was time for a change, it was awful. I had to let staff go and restructure our business model to begin the long, arduous road of building it up again. It was a tough lesson learned. I vowed never to be in that position again.

4) **Monitoring Operations**

Having tools, metrics, procedures and systems in place to monitor the key areas of your business is like going to the doctor for a checkup. They allow you to spot potential red flags before they become fatal flaws and help you recognize problem areas so corrective actions can be taken.

Many companies fail simply because ownership did not have a feel on the pulse of their own business.

5) **Delegating Tasks**

Running a catering company/restaurant typically comes with a slew of other titles: manager, marketer, administrator, bookkeeper, salesperson, delivery driver, and chef. While it may be part and parcel of running a smaller operation, there are a few important facts to consider:

• Most people excel in some areas, while they struggle or get by in others.

• An individual's time, energy, and resources

are limited.

• It is impossible for one person to know it all.

• When other people are involved, it brings in different perspectives and ideas to the table.

Once you have a system for tracking progress and measuring results, your vision can be defined and focused. When problems or roadblocks present themselves, determine whether they are within your control, or outside your influence? Then begin working to fix what you can.

If they are out your control, accept what you cannot change the current situation. With your team, brainstorm alternative solutions to keep moving forward.

5) Track Sales and Expenses Weekly

Revenue is the lifeblood of any business. You need to know where your finances stand at all times. How much money is coming in vs. going out? Are you spending the way you planned?

If you know the answer to those questions, you can make necessary adjustments as needed by nipping problem issues in the bud.

6) Track Progress

Carefully analyze which direction your business is trending. Ask yourself, "How can this operation become more efficient, and more profitable?"

With your staff, walk thru your establishment as if you were looking at it for the first time. What changes would you make?

7) Poor Accounting

You cannot be in control of your business if you don't know what is going on financially. With bad numbers, or no numbers, a company is flying blind, and it happens more often than you think.

Why? For one, it is a common, and potentially disastrous, misconception that an outside accounting firm hired primarily to do the taxes will keep watch over the business. In reality, that is the job of the chief financial officer, one of the many hats an owner has to wear unless you hire a CFO.

8) Leaving Money on the Table

In an interview with Michael Attias, Founder of Restaurant Catering Systems, he shared, "Restaurants that begin a catering division can generate an additional revenue stream of between 10%-30%, based on their efforts." He also noted, "Since the vast majority of catering related expenses are already being covered by the restaurant, 50% of this additional revenue goes right to the bottom line."

THE BOTTOM LINE

Whether you are making money, losing money, breaking even, or are not sure, don't you want to know the true financial health of your business? If you are not sure about where things stand financially, or if you are losing money stop what you are doing right now, and get help.

Then, implement a record-keeping system, so the days of dumping shoeboxes of invoices at your accountant's office door in the dead of night are over. Taking control back of your business and experiencing it become profitable, or even more profitable, will feel very good.

But don't wait until you're concerned about making payroll next week. I've been called into those situations. At that point, it is usually too late.

EMPLOYEES DON'T QUIT JOBS...

THEY QUIT BOSSES

Research studies by Forbes, Gallup, and Harvard Business Review found that between 50% and 75% of employees quit their jobs because they "don't like their boss."

Wow. Big Number.

Managing a staff effectively is no small task. It requires a skill-set that matures over years, even decades. When any group of personalities is together regularly, conflict is inevitable. It can be a daunting challenge for leaders to navigate these choppy waters.

How you motivate one person may not apply to another. Employee A may need regular guidance whereas Employee B may perform at their peak when allowed lots of autonomy. We work in an environment where oftentimes the unexpected is commonplace. Amidst this organized chaos, skillful supervisors recognize that communicating the same message to different people must sometimes be tailored to individual personalities.

As owner-operators, managers, and supervisors we wear many hats. In a given day, we may play the role of mentor, teacher, psychologist, disciplinarian, decision-maker, fact-finder, problem-solver, motivator and mediator.

To build an exceptional team - Consistency, just as it applies to your products and services is the key. If your staff feels they can rely on you to communicate and interact with them in a consistent manner, you will build trust and loyalty.

If we want our employees to be the "best-they-can-be," we, as leaders, must make the same commitment. As I regularly urge my clients, "Consider your employees as a continual work in progress." The same principle applies to being "the-best-boss-we-can-be. There is no finish line. We are all a work in progress.

Unlike our employees, we don't have the guidance of a manager to assess our performance. As a result, being open-minded and motivated to improve your leadership skills is an important obligation you have to your business, your staff, and your self.

This can include reading and researching the topic (there is plenty of information available), taking a seminar(s), and talking to leaders or human resource professionals from other businesses.

The Harvard Business Review conducted a study entitled: *Things Good Bosses Believe.*

These were some of the findings:

☐"I have a flawed and incomplete understanding of what it feels like to work for me."

☐"One of the most important and difficult parts of my job is to strike the delicate balance between being too assertive and not assertive enough."

☐"I strive to be confident enough for people to see that I am worthy of being in charge, but humble enough to realize that sometimes I am going to be wrong."

☐"One of the best tests of my leadership – and my organization – is how things are handled after people make a mistake."

☐"Because I wield power over others, I am at great risk of acting like an insensitive jerk and not realizing it."

I like the last one in particular. Our words can carry a lot of weight. One sarcastic comment, may keep an employee up at night while you barely remember saying it.

If you want your employees to be enthusiastic, conscientious, and customer service driven, those in charge must cultivate an environment where nothing less is expected. Staff take cues from their supervisors as they set the bar for what is, and what is not acceptable.

Decide what the underlying principles of working for your operation are going to be. Then live, breathe, and enforce them.

Find the balance between empathizing with, and coaching your employees, while creating a culture of high-standards and an unwavering commitment to excellence.

Along with showing appreciation, there are other things you can do to maximize your staff's potential.

These are some suggestions:

Hold Regular Staff Meetings

This is a great format to keep your crew motivated and on track. Staff meetings are a time to reiterate goals, get input and feedback, air-out grievances and acknowledge employees who have gone the extra mile. During the meeting, keep a written log of issues discussed and always maintain a running list of topics for the next meeting.

Understand Strengths and Limitations

Take time to learn and understand each employee's strengths and limitations. Most employees are best suited for specific positions — you can't force what isn't there.

Also, recognize that no one who works for you is you. Stop hoping they will be.

Observe and be Willing to Shake Things Up

Because things have been done a certain way for a long time, doesn't mean it's the best or most efficient method. Regularly observe who is doing what and ask yourself if there is a better way. Besides, sometimes it's good to shake things up.

Involve Your Employees

Remember that your staff can be a tremendous resource for feedback and information. Ask for their ideas or thoughts to make your business better and more efficient. People feel valued when asked for their opinion.

Who knows better about the ins and outs of your operation than those on the front lines? I guarantee that if any of their ideas are implemented, they will have a vested interest in the success of their suggestions.

Prepare and Train, Train, Train

For your employees to have the best shot at success, you need both a training system and a written job description for each position. Great customer service skills are teachable. If you want this reputation for your business, invest the time in thorough training that is documented and updated as needed.

Provide Annual Performance (and self) Evaluations

A format for employees to self-evaluate their performance is a great tool. It gives both them and their supervisor an opportunity to compare their perspectives as part of a formal performance review.

Written, structured annual reviews offer a:

☐Forum for discussing an employee's overall performance, including past successes and future areas of measurable improvement.

☐An opportunity for supervisors to define upcoming goals for the employee and the organization.

☐Tool for the supervisor to determine area(s) where an employee needs additional training.

☐A measureable gauge for wage and benefit

Show Interest In Their Lives

Get to know your staff as people, not only as employees. Are they married? Do they have children? Do they have any difficult circumstances or life situations that you can empathize with and can help accommodate? When is their birthday? When is their work anniversary? What do they enjoy doing when they are not working? Have they had any significant events or accomplishments outside of work?

Showing interest in their lives and acknowledging benchmarks can go a long way to building a loyal team.

THE MAGIC OF LEAVING YOUR COMFORT ZONE

Life Lessons Learned From the Other Side of The World (June 2016)

I am Bohol, a province on the southern side of The Philippines. By the time this column goes live, I will have returned home and been fully re-Americanized. It will be my loss. There is something very special here.

How it Began:

The idea first flickered about a year ago. TheCorporateCaterer.com Leads Program was growing. I was concerned that soon, we'd be struggling to keep up with demand.

The Leads Program is a service we offer thru our community website. Members submit zip codes where they want to peruse new corporate catering business. Our lead generators make hundreds of cold calls on their behalf. The qualified leads (companies that order catering regularly) are available for purchase, in bundles of twenty. It's like hiring a private cold-caller on as "as-needed" basis.

I began researching outside marketing companies that would be qualified to service our specific niche. After an exhaustive six-month search, including some stops and re-starts; I found a call center that seemed the perfect fit.

Their lead generators, (aka "Agents") were the highest skilled, most professional I had interviewed and evaluated. To boot, their parent company held interests in the hotel and restaurant industry. They also wanted an outside (apparently, way outside) perspective on their catering operations.

The perfect fit...except they were located in The Philippines. Truth be told, I had to do a Google search to learn where The Philippines was in the world. (Southeast Asia).

As we worked together over the next few months, it was clear they were the right choice. We saw a noticeable spike of members who were re-ordering leads lists. This is always a good sign. It meant they had success with the first list.

Ahh... Mileage Points:

Itching to see the call center live, meet my lead generators, conduct in-person training, and experience the magic that happens when one leaves their comfort zone, I booked a flight.

The first stop was Bacolod City, home of the call center. There is a twelve-hour time difference between our two worlds. When our lead generators in The Philippines are calling businesses on the East Coast of the United States, their shift is 9 pm to 6 am. When they are calling the West Coast, the shift is midnight to 9 am.

It's an odd feeling working away at 4 am in a buzzing office. Each night/morning, I was so impressed by the energy, enthusiasm, and pride the Agents took in their work.

Teachable? They were like sponges, absorbing every piece of information I presented, continuously asking insightful questions about the art and nuances of getting qualified catering leads.

Every call the Agents make is recorded. Every night/morning, we'd listen to some recordings from the previous day and discuss strategies to common challenges, such as how to get a direct email addresses for the person who orders catering for the office, even when the gatekeeper initially said, "We're not supposed to give that information out."

Catering Cuisine:

Filipino cuisine centers on a combination of sweet, sour and salty tastes. Popular dishes include: lechón (whole roasted pig), longganisa (Philippine sausage), tapa (cured beef), torta (omelette), adobo (chicken and/or pork braised in garlic, vinegar, oil and soy sauce, kaldereta (meat in tomato sauce stew), grilled prawns (the biggest I'd ever seen), and biko (sweet, sticky rice). Some common local ingredients used in cooking are coconuts, saba (a short wide plantain), mangoes, milkfish, and fish sauce.

In general, the food quality was very good. One suggestion I made was to offer more vegetarian side dishes. There is no shortage of starches. The presentation was impressive. The service was simply to best I ever witnessed.

The management team wanted my thoughts on their internal systems and organizational structure. I was able to offer some strategies I think will be helpful.

We talked a lot about the concept of an operations manual, a written step-by-step roadmap for their catering business. Like lots of my clients, they have parts of the daily work flow writing, but not a complete manual.

Interestingly, my suggestion of instituting regular staff meetings with the employees on the front lines (servers, set-up staff), to get their suggestions and air out any issues was met with expressions of confusion.

Over time, it became clear this was a cultural difference between our two societies. As is the case with the Filipino family structure, there is a very clear professional hierarchy that is not crossed.

City of Smiles:

The Philippines is described as both a third-world and a developing country. Regardless, take a five-minute walk in any direction and of the ravages of poverty are impossible to escape.

Weary roadside shacks, which are businesses selling mangoes and iced tea during the day, become shelter and home for families at night. A family of six, with more financial resources, may live in a slightly sturdier structure with two bedrooms, one for the parents, and the other for the children – all the children.

Despite existing in a humid, tropical climate year-round, air conditioning is a luxury most cannot afford.

As the days have spilled into weeks, I have become increasingly fascinated with the manners of the Filipino people. Bacolod City is called, "The City of Smiles." It might as well apply to the entire country. Wherever I go, whatever I do, the consistent politeness and professionalism of The Filipinos is nothing I have ever experienced.

From taxi drivers to young servers in restaurants, to secretly guards patrolling the streets, there is genuine warmth and welcoming that is hard to describe.

I've always preached that the recipe for a great staff is a thorough, thoughtful training program. As of this writing. I have been to four different regions in The Philippines, and it feels as if the whole country has been trained in politeness.

Example: Buying a Cup of Coffee

"Thank you for your purchase today, Sir. I hope you enjoy your coffee and your day as well, in our city. (Apparently, I wasn't blending in with the locals).

"Thank you, I'll be back. My name is Michael."

"We will be happy to see you again, Sir Michael."

"No, just Michael."

"Oh, I am sorry, Sir Michael, that would not be showing you the proper respect in our country."

America could take a page or two from The Filipino playbook in service.

Humanitarianism 101:

Last night, at dinner with new Filipino friends, I got my answer. The whole country is in a sense, trained in politeness. From kindergarten through high school one hour a day is spent teaching...brace yourself, "Being a Good Human Being." No joke.

For twelve years, every day, students are taught the ABC's of manners, politeness, respect, (with an emphasis on respecting your elders), kindness, decency, honesty and responsibility. What a concept...

Additionally, one hour a day is spent teaching English. Actually, "Pilipino" which is a dialect and English are considered the official languages. The fact I can communicate with 90% of the population has made my time here all the richer.

Culturally, the family unit is of utmost importance. It is placed before everything else. It is not uncommon for generations of families to live together.

A common thread of happiness exists here. Last night at dinner, a new friend summed it up like this, "We may not have much, but we don't need much. We have each other, and that is enough."

SUCCESSFUL VENDOR RELATIONSHIPS ARE A TWO-WAY STREET

"When I call a vendor with a problem, I expect them to solve it – quickly. We're a no-nonsense company that delivers the finest customer service experience in our industry. I expect nothing less from our vendors."

> *-Canadian Real Estate Tycoon,*
> *Sol "The Hammer" Shabinsky*
> *My Uncle/Mentor*

To call the caterer/restaurateur and food supplier relationship, a marriage isn't far-fetched. Both sides rely on each other to put food on the table. But like all marriages, one or both sides might take the other for granted, resulting in occasional rough patches.

Good communication is vital to working thru these times. If the business relationship is mutually beneficial, it is worth investing time and effort in the partnership.

Tips to Sustaining Mutually Beneficial Vendor Relationships:

☐Lay Your Cards on the Table

Communicate your business goals as they relate to expectations for your vendors.

If you are striving to grow your catering business, the suppliers you choose should be on board with your vision.

Give them specific examples of your staff delivering exemplary service to your customers. They need to know you expect the same from them.

☐Get it all in Writing

Document the agreed upon terms and conditions including delivery schedule and procedures, pricing policies, product quality expectations, back-up plans, communications, payment terms, and ordering procedures.

☐Communicate Your Assessments

Be direct. If any of your expectations are not being met, let them know. We have all had the frustrating experience of losing a customer, only to later discover the reason(s). Our first thought is, "I wish they had let me know. We could have corrected the issue."

 Your vendors feel the same way. If there is a problem, tell them. There may be an easy solution.

☐Respect Them and their Guidelines

Place your orders on time. Meet the minimums. When they make a delivery, check it in promptly. Offer the delivery person a drink. Address them by their name. If they like you, your account will be a priority.

You want to create an allegiance. If the driver is running late and has to decide who gets the next delivery you want it to be you.

☐Be Reasonable

Miscommunications, unforeseen circumstances, and mistakes are inevitable. Consider how some of your catering customers respond when they are affected by these situations. Respond to your vendors in the matter you most appreciated being treated.

☐Demonstrate Loyalty

If it's not broken, don't fix it. When a vendor has worked hard and done a good job servicing your business, stay with them. When you are loyal to your vendor, especially after a mishap, they will inevitably return the goodwill.

Let their bosses know that their driver and/or service representative are doing a good job for your company. This can pay long-term dividends.

□ **Pay Your Bills**

Pay your invoices on time. If circumstances necessitate a late payment, let them know in advance. Your vendor will appreciate the information, as it may affect their financial obligations.

* * * * *

Albeit an important one, pricing is only one determining factor when choosing a vendor. There are others to consider as well:

□**Product Quality**

The food and product delivered needs to consistently meet your standards. Having worked with many produce companies over the years, I have found the quality of their whole fruit can be the barometer for the quality of their inventory as a whole.

In the event they deliver a case of lettuce that it not satisfactory, how quickly are they able to replace it?

Does your poultry supplier deliver chicken breasts consistent in size and weight? If you carry retail items, does your dairy company have ample sell-by dates stamped on the products you re-sell?

☐Pricing Structure

The best time to negotiate pricing and payment terms is before starting a relationship. Expect to provide information about your current or anticipated ordering volume, as this may affect the proposal. Discuss parameters for how long prices will be guaranteed and/or maximum percentage increases over specific time periods.

Keep in mind; there is nothing wrong with asking any or all of your current suppliers to sharpen their pencils and offer more aggressive pricing across-the-board. If you can shave half-a-percentage point from six vendors, that could be a 3% food cost reduction.

☐Pricing Strategy

Let potential new vendors know that you are shopping around. Under no circumstances divulge what you are currently paying for products they are bidding. There may be a time when you share actual invoices from other vendors with them, but insist they show their hand first. If they ask what you are currently paying, respond, "I'd first like to see the most aggressive pricing you can offer us." Period.

Don't be shy to share that you've been around the block a few times and are all too familiar with the game of "low-balling to get the account, followed by a gradual price increase over time." Let them know that someone on your staff is tasked with tracking all vendors pricing. (Someone should be doing this.) While market conditions will sometimes result in price swings, if they operate under the "reel 'em in at rock-bottom pricing and inch 'em up slowly" strategy, they are wasting your valuable time.

☐Payment Terms

How much time do you need to pay their bills? "Net / 30" is typically the longest term most companies will offer.

If their standard terms are "Net /15" but you require longer, ask if it is negotiable?

What is their policy if you need a couple of additional weeks beyond "terms" on occasion? Will they still deliver to you during these times?

☐Delivery Schedule

Determine if your delivery parameters are within a vendor's capability. If you need fresh bread and bakery items at 5 am every morning, can they guarantee it? For other products, there may be only specific time frames when you can accept deliveries.

How far away are they located? How many delivery trucks do they have on the road? When you need something last minute, will they come through for you?

Consider your vendors an extension of your staff and assume a role in cultivating partnerships with them. You don't want "order-takers."

You want your vendor representative to keep an eye out for new products and menu items that fit your brand and suggest ideas that will help your business grow. They may even pass along information about your competitors.

You want your suppliers, account reps, and delivery drivers to feel a vested interest in your long-term success. Remember...achieving this is a two-way street. And it is smart business.

STAYING TRUE TO YOUR PRODUCT AND YOUR PRICING

I've consulted for restaurateur's who's mentality is:

"I can't have too many customers; I need a line out to the street; the more, the better, the busier, the better; I don't care if they are parties of thirty or single diners; I'll take whatever comes in."

This thought process, however, can be counter-productive to the financial health of your catering business. I remember attending Catersource seminars and conferences, and when a caterer mentioned a five hunfdred-person party, the crowd sighed longingly as they knew the large event's monetary value. But sometimes we unwittingly hand these events over to someone else, and I'll tell you how that happens.

The Nice Guy (Who Sometimes Finishes Last)

It's Monday in January, and nothing is going on. Someone calls and says,

"I need lunch for people on Wednesday. Can you do this?"

You reply, "Sure, what do you need?"

"Well, I need fifty need box lunches, but I have a problem."

"What's that?"

"I have a maximum budget of $550."

You look at Wednesday and see there are only four orders booked. You know you 50 box lunches at $11 per person would equate to a 15% discount off your menu price.

It's a quiet time of year, a colleague recently advised, "You put money in the bank—not percentages," and you say, "Sure, we can do this."

What Happened Next

The customer really liked the meal and wanted to arrange a standing order every week, but only if it could be at the discounted price.

The Big Event

Some months later you found out the same customer booked a five hundred-person event, with a competitor of yours. When you asked why you had not been at least considered for the big event, your customer responded,

"Wow, I'm really sorry. It seemed like you were such an expert at my smaller lunches, I thought that was your specialty. I didn't even know you did large and more expensive events. I can let the committee know, and maybe we will consider you in the future."

A good reminder of the adage, "Perception is Reality."

What You Did

By undercutting yourself on the fifty-person lunch, you branded yourself as a small caterer who accepted, even welcomed inexpensive orders. If you are discounting an order, make sure your customer knows you are doing it.

Do be careful, because the more you cut your pricing, the more requests you will get to do so, and the prime events will go to the branded big event caterer.

Yes, there are times, especially when you are bidding big job against other caterers when you might take the size of the order into consideration when pricing it – but honor and stand behind your product.

A COLD, COLD FEELING

Although cold-calling prospective customers isn't fun, it works. During the early stage of our catering business, I identified possible new clients and simply asked if they had ever used a caterer.

One February morning I called a large local heating supply business. They wholesaled HVAC units, and I knew they hosted lots of day-long classes for their customers and their in-house sales staff.

Got Lucky

The person who answered the phone also happened to be in charge of ordering catering for the office. She told me I had called at the right time because they had two important meetings that week for sixty guests each and needed food.

She further explained that they liked a certain menu and wanted the same thing both days since the guests would be different. One of the main items they requested was chicken salad. The conversation ended as I was told that we would be given a chance.

Let's Do It

I excitedly told my wife that we had gotten a new customer; we wanted to do everything possible to make a great impression.

We had a killer recipe for chicken salad that we made with grilled chicken breasts, and we couldn't wait to get started.

We Were Ready

Even though this new customer had ordered a rather pedestrian level of food (we thought), we spent hours making it as upscale as possible.

Everything was beautifully garnished and perfectly packaged. I delivered the order myself, went back to the kitchen, waited until sufficient time had passed, and called the customer to see what they thought.

Not What I Wanted to Hear

Here's how the call went:

Me: "Hi, Mrs. Johnson. Just calling to see how lunch went today."

Her: "Well, most of it was OK, but that chicken salad was a problem."

Me: "Wow, we spent hours preparing it; what was the issue?"

Her: "I wanted "normal" chicken salad, chunks of chicken with celery and mayonnaise. in it. We didn't want any grilled nonsense."

Me: "Umm...

Her: "You are bringing us food tomorrow. I'll give you one more chance."

Plan B

I was upset, but I knew what to do. Our produce vendor sold this boring chicken salad that was chicken + mayonnaise and not much else. We had rejected the product in the past, but I figured if this customer wanted what they considered, "normal" chicken salad, that's what they would get.

We ordered 20 pounds, dumped it in a mixing bowl, added mayonnaise and celery, put it a big serving bowl, and off it went.

Guess What?

Here's how the next day's call went:

Me: "Mrs. Johnson – Hi, it's Richard. How was your lunch today?"

Her: "Young man, that was exactly what I was looking for. It was great. Call me next week, and we'll set up some more orders."

Moral of the Story

Never try to force your personal tastes upon a customer. Listen to what they want, and give it to them, regardless of your personal preference.

Very early in my career, I was responsible for ordering candy and chips for a thirty slot vending machine in a corporate break room.

My boss at the time gave me great advice. "I always want you to order ten products that you would never buy for yourself. Just because you don't like Peppermint Patties or Snickers Bars or Reduced-Fat Potato Chips, doesn't mean the same is true for many other people."

*   *   *   *   *

"REAL DEAL" LEADS, LEADS, LEADS

Remember, we at The Corporate Caterer have a great leads program that puts you a step ahead of your competition. We offer "real deal leads."

Our lead generators make between 500-750 cold calls to compile a list of companies that order catering regularly, and the contact information of the person who places the orders.

You give us zip codes where you want to pursue new business and we take care of the heavy lifting from there. Check out our website for more information, www.TheCorporateCaterer.com

P.S. That HVAC company became a top account for many, many years.

Who You Gonna Call?

There's nothing like being so busy you don't know how you're going to get all the food out, and delivered on time. This is a good problem/challenge to have. You want to be in this situation.

What happens when business is slow, and you are very concerned about making ends meet financially?

The DNA of entrepreneurs are different. Our businesses are many times our lives, but our employees do not feel the same way. One thing I have noticed over the years is the mental and physical toll that results from the continuous pursuit of money. While payday is a great day for our staff, it may not be so friendly to us since we need to fund it.

It's not hard to see the diametrically opposed perceptions of owners and employees. If we as owners are not careful, the never-ending need for cash can cause us to react in ways that send a signal indicating we may not be the best bosses to work for, such as:

1) We develop a short fuse and become easily aggravated over trivial things.

2) We become upset if someone is a few minutes late for even a good reason.

3) We subconsciously blame employees for getting sick.

4) We develop little tolerance for error.

5) We constantly micro-manage and want to leave our personal stamp on all facets of the business.

6) We are reluctant to grant time-off for good reasons like doctor's appointments and family emergencies.

7) We become distrustful of everyone.

The Opposite

When employees are hard to find, we look for ways to keep the ones we have happy. On an extremely busy day, everyone will need to step up, and no one is going to want to help you if frankly, you always act like a jerk.

Consider points one through seven and do the opposite; then watch the positive effect this will have on your entire operation.

IF YOU LOOKED UP

"CATERING WAR STORY"

IN THE DICTIONARY...

In our early catering days, we were lucky enough to land a 1000-person casual buffet dinner event for our municipality's city council. At that time, we were catering out of a diner-style restaurant that lacked convection ovens.

Some of our events were summer picnics and tailgate parties where we cooked much of the food on grilles at the site; the fact that we didn't have a lot of oven space didn't usually wasn't an issue, except this time.

Our client loved our vegetable lasagna. I should say Stouffer's Vegetable Lasagna and wanted us to serve it to the 1000 guests. I knew two critical things about this product because we had used it many times:

It would stay frozen for a long time even at room temperature.

Conversely, it would stay hot for hours if stored in the original cardboard cases after cooking.

It was available at Sam's Club, so the plan was to pick it up there, take it home to cook it in two shots--we had two ovens at our house--quickly put it back in the cases, take it to the event and load it into wire rack chafers as needed.

We had a picnic booked earlier in the day, and we had one truck.

This was the plan: Help set up the picnic, leave my staff there, go pick up the lasagna at Sam's Club, (we had pre-arranged with Sam's to have what we needed, ready for pick-up), return to the picnic to help break down and clean up, travel to my house, cook the lasagna, and take it to the council event site where our additional staff was setting up and cooking the other menu items.

The picnic went off without a hitch. I made the pickup at Sams, and headed back the picnic site with twenty cases of Stouffer's Vegetable Lasagna in the back of the truck, to help break-down.

In our early days, we counted on picnic sites that offered a large barrel or designated area where still-hot charcoal could be dumped. Unfortunately, this picnic had been held at an office building, and while there were dumpsters galore, there was no safe place to dispose of the charcoal.

We did the next best thing and put the dying and almost extinguished coals in covered aluminum pans, placed them on the truck with the rest of the stuff, and got on the freeway.

Things were going as scheduled until I saw an aluminum pan cover become airborne, and then another, and another... As if that wasn't enough, the nice breeze created as we traveled 60 miles per hour on the freeway conveniently woke up the dead charcoal and sparks began to fly.

I made it to the freeway exit ramp near my house, but when I looked in the rear view mirror, the back of the pick-up was engulfed in flames. The sparks from the rejuvenated charcoal had lit the lasagna cases on fire.

Other drivers were pointing at me while they frantically beeped their horns, and I was worried the fire department would be called, turn their hoses on my truck and ruin my lasagna.

I quickly pulled over on a busy street and did a dance in the pickup bed as I stamped out the fire. But as soon as I started for home—a mere five blocked away—the fire reignited.

Now I was driving down a residential street with a cargo of fire. I made it to my house, got the garden hose, and put out the fire. My plastic bedliner was partially melted, but the lasagna was OK.

I salvaged whatever cardboard lasagna cases I could. I still needed to keep the product hot after cooking and proceeded to load the lasagna into my home ovens. Miraculously, the big event was a success.

I never did get the truck's bed liner repaired, however, because the melted spots were always a reminder to me that especially in the catering business if something can go wrong, it might.

IS THIS THE REASON YOUR BUSINESS IS NOT GROWING?

Chances are, you are running your own business for one, or more of these reasons:

- You worked for a similar business and thought we could do a better job.
- You became tired of working for someone else.
- An opportunity appeared, and we took it.
- You lost your job and never wanted that to happen again.
- Entrepreneurship was prevalent in your families, so it was natural for you to start a business.
- You had a passion for something and wanted to bring it to others.
- You wanted the potential of unlimited income.

Employees are Not Like You

As the owner, you have a unique world-view regarding your business. It's *everything* to you. You always think about it, you dream about it, and you constantly worry about it.

Your employees, however, do not. It's not theirs; it's merely their job, and they may not love the food business like you do. They may not get excited about a 37-order drop-off catering day, while you can't wait for that day to begin.

I remember one busy day at my first restaurant, as we were packing to-go orders, I found an extra order of onion rings and quickly realized that someone had received fries instead of rings.

It was too late as the customer already had left with their bag of food, and I said my expeditor, "Hey, that customer didn't get their onion rings—you gave them fries instead.

She said, "Fries, Rings...at least the got something." I was appalled that one of my employees did not have the same passion for getting things right that I had, but it was a proverbial wake-up call.

Your Challenge

You need to find a way to balance these opposing viewpoints. First, recognize and accept that while you may occasionally get lucky, many of your employees will not come to you with the same drive and enthusiasm that you possess. You have to be ready to deal with this positively instead of negatively.

I could have let the rings vs. fry situation forever taint my feelings about employees. I could have gone down the road that many business owners follow as they fully expect their employees to act badly and make mistakes.

Remember the movie Raising Arizona where the furniture store owner is asked if he has any disgruntled employees? His answer was, "they're employees; of course they are disgruntled."

If that's the way you feel, then you will probably have a store full of unhappy and uncaring workers, and then you will be the most stifling aspect of your business.

Hire carefully. Train thoroughly. Lead by example. Still, every person you hire will not work out. Once you realize someone is not a good fit for your business, cut bait. Quickly.

Don't allow their negative energy to infiltrate the environment you are working hard to cultivate.

LET IT SNOW!

Oh, the joys winter (for those affected) can bring us. There is nothing like the inevitable few days (or more), every year that snow starts falling, and falling and falling some more, wreaking havoc for all.

Canceled orders, late vendor deliveries, a making our deliveries safely and timely. Sometimes, that's only the beginning.

Monitoring the Weather

If you own a restaurant, you know that the weather can be your mortal enemy at times. Early in my career, I owned breakfast and lunch restaurant close to a big law school.

My place totally relied on walk-in traffic. If it was sunny and nice, we could have a great lunch, but rain at noon represented a dollar loss that would never be recouped.

When I became a corporate caterer, I was happy that for once, I didn't have to live and die with the weather. Rain, wind, and cold didn't bother me as customers had their events and meetings regardless.

I could casually watch the nightly weather report and not fear that a steady rain would cost me hundreds of dollars.

Not Quite

The holiday season, unfortunately, brought the weather quickly back in focus. Since we were in Boston, true winter could start anytime in late October or early November.

To be honest, I used to enjoy temperatures between 35 and 42 degrees since our vehicles would be natural refrigerators. We didn't have to ice any cold food or find enough insulated Cambros and coolers to handle a large event.

Sub-freezing

If it got really cold, our trays and platters would still be OK in the unheated truck (these were the very early years), for a short period, and we were comfortable navigating these temperature issues. Snow, however, was another thing altogether.

Bad Weather on the Busiest Day

In the Fall of 2008, when everything hit the fan, there was one silver lining for our corporate catering business. Companies that traditionally threw swanky Saturday night holiday bashes for their employees (and guests), toned things down considerably. They were often replaced by nice lunches, in the office, during the week.

It just so happened that this year, our busiest day of the season was on a collision course with about a foot of forecasted snow.

Quick Recovery

In Boston, we were used to snow, and even a foot depending what time it started would not be that big a deal. The plows would be out all night and streets would be in relatively decent shape the next morning.

This time the snow started at 4:00 a.m. and was peaking at 11:00 a.m., just when we had to get all of the food out.

Warned the Staff

I let my staff know I expected them to plan accordingly. I suggested they leave for work an hour earlier than usual. They would need time to brush snow off their car hoods and scrape ice off their windows. Then, the inevitably slower commute would begin.

I knew that even though bad weather was on the way, our customers would still want their food, and I was right, as we received four or five calls confirming that not only was our food still needed—it was expected to be delivered on time.

We were fine in the kitchen. We were able to load up our four SUV's and get them out, but it took four us to push the loaded trucks through two-foot snow drifts and get them on their way.

A Different Business

If ever we wished that we were office workers in a nice warm building it was on those days. And yes, we got the food out, the customers were happy, and we got paid. Not delivering the food was not an option, so we fought through the adverse conditions. It's our job. It's what we do.

OVERTIME BLUES

Some of my of my coaching and consulting clients pay their "management" staff a salary and their "non-management" staff an hourly rate. Others pay their entire staff an hourly rate. Hourly employees are entitled to time-and-a-half after working forty hours in a week.

Until recently, a Department of Labor rule said that all you had to do was make sure that all "managers" made at least $23,660 and you could require them to work over 40 hours without being paid overtime.

Not Fair

President Obama along with many labor leaders felt this was inequitable. A Pizza Hut manager being paid $35,000 per year, for example, might average 80 hours per week.

That would mean that he or she would earn $8.41 per hour. Obama pushed the Department of Labor to raise the overtime salary threshold to $47,476. This meant that anyone one made less than that amount was entitled to overtime at time-and-a-half. This change was set to occur on December 1st, 2016.

Then This Happened

A federal judge blocked a Department of Labor rule on overtime pay that made more than 4 million private-sector workers eligible for mandatory extra pay or time off.

U.S. District Judge Amos Mazzant of the Eastern District of Texas, whom President Obama appointed, imposed a nationwide injunction against the rule at the request of 21 states, the U.S. Chamber of Commerce and other organizations.

Business groups cheered the decision as another rebuke of the Obama administration's penchant for regulation and for extending executive power.

'The Labor Department's overtime changes are a reckless and aggressive overreach of executive power, and retailers are pleased with the judge's decision,' said David French, the National Retail Federation's senior vice president for government relations.

The judge said the Labor Department regulation exceeded the authority granted it by Congress, which he said gave Labor the right to define which workers are considered salaried but only based on the duties they performed, not by how much they made."

So, What Should You Do Now

If you were worried that you would soon have to pay Becky—your $45,000 manager—overtime when she worked those long holiday weeks you can relax.

The federal courts have blocked the new regulation, and it may not take effect for a long time, if at all, since the Trump administration is unlikely to lobby for any overtime rule changes.

But That's Not the Point

I always paid overtime. I wanted my employees to benefit when they had to work extra hours. If my $14.00 per hour cooks had to work long and hard for a stretch, at least they knew that they would be making $21.00 per hour for any hours after forty hours. They loved overtime, and the busier we became, the happier they were.

Rethink It

While some may legitimately utilize and follow the regulations that allow you to employ some managers paid by salary and therefore ineligible for overtime,

I 've always felt that as long as we were in the black, my business should not only benefit me and my family, but also my dedicated staff and their families. Hiring great employees is something I place a premium on. Without a solid team, success is a daunting challenge.

Remember Who Makes Your Business Run

We were always looking to be more efficient, and while we served the best food possible, we didn't hesitate to experiment with new suppliers and/or new products. One item that we were not satisfied with was bagels.

You should never serve a day-old bagel, and producing them from scratch is a complicated process. While we eventually found a par-baked bagel we could work with, we many times purchased fresh bagels at a local Bruegger's location.

Analyze It

Some days I made the morning bagel pickup, and I used the opportunity to learn about the Bruegger's operation. I watched as a lone cook sweated over a big kettle as he dropped raw bagels into boiling water.

Simultaneously he trayed just boiled bagels, adding poppy seeds, sesame seeds or other toppings; he then loaded just-boiled bagels into a large conveyer oven.

Next, he removed perfectly the baked product as the conveyor shelves moved to the top. He never stopped the rotating oven shelves, and I knew I was watching a highly skilled and specialized worker.

He Was It

One day I went to pick up our order at 6:00 a.m. and the front door was locked. The bagel cook hadn't shown up that day—maybe he was sick, had car trouble, overslept, who knows—but without him, everything stopped.

The first person who came to work that day probably called the manager and alternative arrangements were undoubtedly made.

Nonetheless, the store opened late, and I'm sure the rest of the employees didn't have a fun day.

Pay That Guy (or Gal)

Regardless how matter how many managers, supervisors and assistant managers worked at that location, no one was more important than the bagel maker.

Not only did he have to get up at 3:30 am, he was solely responsible for having the product ready on time. In my mind, on the day that I couldn't pick up my order, I felt that the bagel store should be paying their most important employee $50.00 per hour.

Not Going to Happen

Of course, they wouldn't do that because a bagel cook was probably paid like a dishwasher. Maybe he couldn't speak English or handle money, and he probably could only do one thing—albeit the most important.

Me Neither

OK, I'll confess. At first, I didn't pay my dishwasher very much either, but when he didn't show up, my kitchen was a disaster.

Try coming out of a thirty-five-order lunch with pots, pans and trays stacked three feet high with no one to run them through the machine. It would take us hours to recover from a situation like that.

Change

After a few of those days, I made it a point to ensure that my dishwasher knew I appreciated him and valued his work. In fact, I think the same applies to your entire staff. As long as you can afford to, walk the kitchen and hand out $50 bills after a successful, extra-busy week, offer some paid time-off, make someone's car payment, distribute gift cards, or do whatever you want to show your gratitude. From what I learned on many days, I would rather lose a manager than a great dishwasher.

Franchised Corporate Caterers

While I was running my restaurant, I was keenly aware of any fast food chains ready to open nearby. This happened a few times, and we still survived, but it was a constant worry. When we transitioned to 100 percent corporate catering, I would often say, "well, this business has its challenges, but a business like corporate drop-off catering is so hands-on and localized that it would be very difficult for anyone to develop a successful franchise model."

Pretenders

A few times, I saw franchised operations that called themselves corporate caterers, but upon closer examination, it became clear that they were merely delivery services; they didn't produce their food, rather simply delivered the products of other caterers.

Alonti Catering Kitchen

One day I had a meeting with my lawyer, and when I arrived, I saw that the office had ordered food for another lunch meeting. Never missing an educational opportunity, I quickly found the administrative assistant who had ordered the food and asked a few questions:

Me: "Do you often order food for lunch meetings?"

Admin: "About twice a month."

Me: "Where do you normally get it from?"

Admin: "Up until now, mostly restaurants."

Me: "How did that go?"

Admin: " The food was OK, but a lot of times it just came in random boxes and aluminum pans. We had to set it up ourselves, and usually we had to have our own paper supplies, or were missing a salad dressing, or a special request had been ignored."

Me: "So, who brought that nice-looking food today?"

Admin:" Someone cold-called our office from Alonti Catering Kitchen and sent me a coupon for a future order. Eventually I tried them, and honestly, I'm going to use them again. Ordering was easy, the food came on-time, everything looked great, and the driver set it all up for us."

Testimonial

I was curious about the company that had delivered/catered lunch that day and did some research. Apparently, Alonti started as a mom and pop catering operation in Houston and now has franchises in California, Texas, and Illinois.

I will tell you that the make-your-own-sandwich buffet I saw was formidable. Appropriate items were branded and special printed. Alonti used a minimum of black plastic trays and instead placed the food in customized rectangular boxes with lids. This made it easy to transport, and since the food was artistically prepared, it looked great. Even the ice bucket was unique—a waxed movie popcorn-like container that was covered with the Alonti logo and colors.

Alonti is in three states, and I'm sure looking to expand into more. They have figured out how to standardize all of their business practices; undoubtedly everything is recorded in a manual that covers all eventualities.

Most importantly, they understand exactly what is necessary to succeed in corporate catering: serve great-looking food on-time for a fair price.

What You Need to Do

If you are in a larger city in Texas, Illinois or California, Alonti may already be your competitor. If you are not, I urge you to look at their website and understand how they have standardized their operation so completely that they can open a store in any city that meets their business parameters.

The Alonti experience just reinforces what I have already shared with you previously:

1) Pay attention to your branding.
2) Ensure that your food looks great.
3) Have an easy-to-understand ordering system.
4) Have a great online presence.
5) Always set up all orders.
6) Don't be late!

The Corporate Caterer can work directly with you and your team to create a custom operations manual. I could talk for hours about the value written standard operating procedures (SOP).

A 3-ring binder, (and of course a digital version), with everything documented about how your business is run, step-by-step is worth its weight is gold.

From how the phones are answered, to what an "assorted" sandwich platter consists of, regardless of who is producing it, to how deliveries are set up, this information should be accessible to all your employees.

This is the heart and soul that enables you to offer a consistent product and service. It is the most significant component to create the golden goose of corporate drop-off catering –

REPEAT BUSINESS.

For more information how we can assist you create your own often talked about but rarely executed operations manual, contact us anytime.

YOUR WORST NIGHTMARE

Imagine waking up to a call from your local health department informing you that scores of guests that attended an event you catered two days ago are reporting that they are sick. Food safety is one of your greatest responsibilities, and if you don't ensure that the correct guidelines are being followed, you can end up in an absolute crisis.

The most recent example was when Chipotle was forced to shut down its 2,000 locations for a day because an outbreak of their food had given people E. coli and salmonella. Will Chipoltle survive the crisis? Probably. Will there be a longer-term damage to their brand? Quite possibly.

Danger Signs

My colleague Richard Radbil reports from Austin, Texas about some practices he recently witnessed first-hand that could lead to disaster:

The Myth of Gloves and Food Safety

"I was at a large hotel that has a cool hamburger outlet with a trailer-like look that opens up to the street. Their menu is simple—burgers, grilled chicken, and a few sides. The meats are kept in separate drawers under the flat top and are cooked to order. All of the cooks wear gloves, but,

1) I saw a cook grab a thawed and dripping raw chicken breast with his gloved hand. He then wiped his gloved hand on a towel (!) and proceeded to reach for a raw burger that he placed on the grill.

   This is a classic case of cross-contamination as any bacteria from the chicken were now on the burger. Maybe everyone gets lucky, and the bacteria are killed if the burger is cooked properly, but would you take that chance?

2) I witnessed another cook flipping a raw chicken breast and then using the same spatula to take a cooked burger off of the grill. Since the chicken breast was only cooked on one side, bacteria could have gone right to the burger, and since the burger was then off the grill, any bacteria could have survived the reduced heat.

3) I watched as a cook with gloved hands took an order from a customer since the order-taker was nowhere to be seen. The cook handled money, wiped his gloved hands on a towel and reached into the meat drawer for more product.

4) At another outlet, I saw a cook open a bag of thawed tenderloin tips, reach into the bag to grab handfuls of meat, and put them on the grill to cook. While the meat was cooking, the worker started assembling bowls of food without changing her gloves."

Recipe for Disaster

I preach about the perils of micro-management, but food safety is one area where you need to get into your kitchen and see what is going on. While Chipotle--although seriously injured-- will probably survive, you may not.

No one is going to want to use the caterer who made everyone sick. The first thing you need to do, if you haven't already, is to become ServSafe Certified.

Take the manager course, and you will learn:

The Importance of Food Safety

Good Personal Hygiene

Time and Temperature Control

Preventing Cross-Contamination

Cleaning and Sanitizing

Safe Food Preparation

Receiving and Storing Food

Methods of Thawing, Cooking, Cooling and Reheating Food

HACCP (Hazard Analysis and Critical Control Points)

* * * * *

Food Safety Regulations

Then, make it mandatory for all of your employees to take the employee course. I assure you that no one will ever look at food preparation the same way.

Liability

Every business has liability concerns. Accountants could make a mistake that causes IRS problems, the oil change shop could forget to refill a car with fresh oil, and the store that doesn't shovel snow in front of its entrance could cause someone to slip and fall.

Our potential food safety issues are more complicated. We have to be aware of numerous different aspects when we handle food. We have to police our vendors, our cooks, our drivers, our clean-up crews and more. One false move on any given day can put us out of business.

IT'S YOUR FAULT

One of the most frequent questions I'm asked is, "Why am I not doing more business? My catering volume seems to be stuck at (for example) $400,000 and no matter what I do, sales just do not increase."

This invariably leads to a wide-ranging discussion about sales strategy, expanded menus, market awareness, advertising, social media presence and more. The actual answer to this question, however, is a lot easier. The real reason that your sales are not increasing could be you!

Are You Ready?

As my company was growing, I was faced with a time-off dilemma. Since our business was mostly corporate, Monday through Friday was a busy time. If we added some weekend events, I would just work seven days per week.

Family Activity

One year in May a close family friend was due to graduate from an out of state university. This was a big deal, and there was no way I was missing it. The problem was that I would have to leave on a Thursday night and miss Friday's business.

Since at that time I had a hand in EVERY catering order that left our kitchen, and because I had not yet even considered training anyone to take my place, I had to figure how the Friday food would get out without me.

I Wanted a Slow Day!

My solution was to ask our favorite server, a highly competent person who would find us extra help when we had an event that needed more staff, if she could work that Friday and supervise the kitchen. We were doing about $600,000 annually at the time and Fridays were notoriously slower, so for once I was hoping we would have a slow day.

She Said OK

Jenny was happy to oblige, and on Wednesday I started prepping her for Friday's business. We had five orders at the time, and I exquisitely choreographed Jenny's every move. On Thursday morning two more orders were called in; I rationalized that this day would still work and I left to get a haircut. Since I had at least ten tasks still hanging,

I had allocated exactly 40 minutes for my haircut including travel to the barbershop.

Impatient

I arrived at the barber's place, and he was running a half-hour behind. I was so busy I wouldn't wait, and I drove back to the kitchen and knocked two more things off my list; I then went back to get my hair cut. Of course, another two orders came in, and now the Friday that would have been slightly busy for me was now going to be extremely challenging for Jenny.

I Still Got on the Plane

Regardless of my insecurities, since I was well aware that if something could go wrong, it might, I left on Thursday night. I tried to avoid contacting Jenny until after lunch on Friday, but a cell phone call from a slightly agitated customer wondering where his food was interrupted my self-imposed relaxation time at the hotel pool. After a quick call to Jenny I had heard the whole sad, sad story:

Really?

"Well, another order came in this morning. I got my husband Bill to deliver it, but he locked his keys in the car with the food. Sycso was an hour late, and we needed the tuna fish for the sandwiches platter, so we were scrambling a bit. By the time I got out to Bill's car we were a few minutes late. Everything's OK, though, so you have a relaxing time and don't worry about anything!"

What I Learned

After a follow-up phone call to the previously worried customer and following a conversation with Jenny I was able to ascertain that no real damage had been done. I quickly understood, however, that if I was ever going to be ready for prime-time, I had lots of work to do. I realized that not being ready to leave my kitchen for even one day was negatively influencing the way my employees, current and potential customers, and even vendors were perceiving my business.

Count Your Blessings

Depending on where you live, summer may be a slower time, and you can't wait for the post-labor-day business increase, or possibly you are burnt out—literally and figuratively, from cooking lots of brats and burgers in the sun at company picnics and baseball tailgate parties.

Wistfully Walking

When we launched a full-service catering division, (run by someone else), I worked some weekend events. I remember Saturday nights when I would be heading to a late event; I would pass a nice outdoor restaurant patio and longingly gaze at the people laughing, eating homemade nachos chips with fresh guacamole and drinking margaritas.

It was Saturday, and they didn't have to go back to work until Monday. Later, while I was unloading messy post-event catering trucks, those happy diners were undoubtedly in bed with no plans to get up early. Maybe, I thought, I should just get out of this nasty business and get a job with regular hours and less stress.

Wise Words

My CPA would always tell me, however, that there was no way I could ever work for anyone else. "You have too many perks and too much freedom," he said. "You also have the ability to produce unlimited income, and people, who have regular jobs just do not have that." And, of course, he was right.

Examples

1) One of my clients sold his catering business and got a food service job at a major university. While it was refreshing for about five minutes, he quickly grew unhappy as his years of catering experience were ignored, front-line employees were institutionally treated poorly, his income was less than he'd had grown accustomed to, (and fixed), and he was prohibited from innovating anything. He's back in the catering business now.

2) Another former client still cannot get used to the fact that he has to ask someone if he can go to the dentist during working hours. When he ran his own business, he merely made the appointment and made sure it was in the afternoon when nothing was going

on. Now he has to fill out a form and email three people for permission.

3) A third catering alumnus is stressed because no matter how hard she works her paycheck amount is still the same. There is no way for her to have a "good month." She has nothing to look forward to.

Be My Guest

There's an old but still amazingly perceptive book called Be My Guest by Conrad Hilton that I highly recommend. Hilton Hotels used to give these books away to every guest, and you can now buy it for almost nothing at Amazon. It tells the Hilton hotel story through the eyes of its founder, Conrad Hilton, who built his hotel chain by conquering adversity. The point here is the Mr. Hilton knew he had to be in business. All he wanted was a business - something he could own and develop. He knew that true wealth could only be gained from being an owner, not an employee.

And that's where you are now. Everything is in place for you to be wildly successful, and all you have to do is remember that you will be eating homemade nachos chips with fresh guacamole and drinking margaritas—maybe just not today.

Your hard work will be rewarded because you have the power to make things happen that regular working people do not.

HOW IS YOUR CATERING ETIQUETTE?

Mike Roman, founder of Catersource, knew that he would have clients from all segments of the catering industry, and he was always careful to be inclusive.

When Mike talked about phone etiquette, for example, he prefaced his remarks by explaining that he understood that some caterers answered the phone from the kitchen as they were actively working to get the food out. While some owners had moved out of the trenches and into an office, Mike realized that many were not there yet.

That Was Me

I was one of those who stayed in the kitchen for a good portion of my career. During one of our many conversations, I asked Mike what he thought was the best way to answer incoming calls. He said, "Just say, 'catering, can I help you?'" I liked that idea's directness and simplicity, and it stuck with us.

Problem Was

Instead of saying, "good afternoon, ABC Catering Company, how may I help you?" I was now free to cut that lengthy greeting to a few words. The problem was, I talked fast anyway, and this allowed me to speak even more quickly. More than a few times this happened:

Me: "Catering, can I help you?"

Caller: "Hi, is this a bad time?"

Me: "No, I can talk."

Caller: "You just seem really busy, and maybe this is a bad time."

Me: "No, sorry I gave you that impression. How

can I help you?"

Caller: "Well, I'd like some ordering information."

Couldn't Get Over It

At times along the way to $2 million in sales, our company became stuck at a certain volume level. At first, I couldn't understand why, for example, if we were doing $800,000 we weren't able to easily move to $900,000. Then, the revelation struck me, and I finally figured it out.

I was the reason. By not taking the time to answer the phone calmly, I was communicating to potential customers that we were too busy to take any more business.

Whether this happened subliminally or blatantly doesn't matter. I was giving the impression that we were stressed—may even too occupied to handle a potential customer's new order.

Maybe they called back later, maybe they called

someone else, or maybe they gave us the small orders and saved the big ones for someone they felt could handle it more efficiently. Regardless, my unconscious hurriedness on the phone was not helping instill customer confidence.

With Everyone Else Too

Next, I realized that I was giving off this vibe to everyone including my employees and vendors.

If everyone picked up on the fact that I was hurried, stressed and worried, no wonder our business had a hard time growing.

The Fix

I knew I was still going to be intense—and I wasn't changing my personality—but I now understood that I needed a calmer person on the phone. After I had delegated that task, I had a little more time for other things, and at least I was able to present a less-rushed and more-in-control image to everyone around me. The next step was the $1 million sales mark, and we got there and surpassed it.

WANT IT ALL?
BE CAREFUL!

Old School Business Consultants

Have you ever hired a "general business consultant?" They usually have a laundry list of easy solutions to difficult problems and one of their favorites deals with the continual need for more business. If your question is, "How can I get more business?" one of the answers will be, "Mine your current customers for all of the orders you can get." While this may make sense to you at first, be aware that in some circumstances, it *may* be penny-wise and pound-foolish.

Not Just Box Lunches

We had many customers that only ordered box lunches from us. Occasionally, when I took a delivery myself, I would meet a competing caterer's driver in the parking lot or on the elevator. Yes, we consistently got the box lunch orders, but they always did the cocktail parties, plated dinners and other more upscale events for that same customer.

I'm sure you have been faced with that situation, and if you asked a general business consultant what to do, he would say, "Make an appointment with the decision maker and get that business. XYZ Data is already a customer of yours, so the selling job will certainly be easier than cold-calling."

He's right, but it may not always be what's best in the long run. I've always followed these two guiding principles:

1) I'd rather do *regular* business with a company for a long time, rather than *all* their business for a much shorter time.

2) NEVER be in a position that if you lose your biggest client – you're screwed. At any given time, I never want to see that our biggest client represents more than 10% of our total business.

Variety

Your company is in your customer's catering *rotation* for an important reason: They want food that tastes different. It doesn't matter that your tacos, chicken parmesan, BBQ, hamburger bar, salad display and continental breakfasts are each unique menu items.

They still, however, come from the same kitchen and taste like your food. If you're at one office constantly, they may tire of your product and look elsewhere. Or, something worse could happen.

Exclusive Looked Good Then

In my early catering years, I thought it would be great to get all the business a customer had. I wanted their hot breakfasts, sandwich platter lunches, awards dinners, holiday parties, picnics and even afternoon snacks.

I didn't want to see another caterer near their building, and if they ordered from someone else, I took it as a personal insult. I never considered the down side of this approach until this happened to me:

One Mistake

We had worked hard to garner all of a major accounting firm's business. We were there five days a week; we had our own storage area, and we cruised along past the $100,000 sales mark (for this customer only), as this company became our best client at the time.

We did everything including private events at the CEO's home. Then, we suffered a miscommunication, lost an order and blew an event. Unfortunately, it was for a high-level meeting with associates who were flown in from across the country.

One of these associates was our customer's national VP of sales, and he was so upset that the meeting, in his eyes, was ruined, he actually demanded that we be fired.

All of the built-up goodwill evaporated, and we were gone, and we couldn't do anything about it. Whether or not the punishment fit the crime, (ps...it did not, in my opinion), Guess what? My opinion didn't matter. The people paying us were calling the shots.

Complacent

Since we always had this account to fall back upon, we had not done a good job of nurturing new business. Frankly, we were so busy with this company that we didn't have time for anything else, and it dented our cash flow for quite a while.

What We Learned

From that day on, we got as many customers as we could, and didn't worry if we met other caterers along the way. If we made a mistake and it cost us a client, we had others who would take their place.

We were happy that our customers could taste a variety of food and had something to compare our stellar service and wonderful cuisine to. We watched as other caterers made the errors since we were able to concentrate on what we did right.

Counter Intuitive

Sure, it's important to have big volume customers, but you need to be careful. So many times we are told to mine our customers for everything we can get. While this certainly is not a "bad decision," there is a flip side to consider. This, however, is the kind of real-world advice you get from those who have been there.

Is Bigger Always Better?

I have spent a lot of time analyzing why some businesses grow and why some seem to be stuck, and my favorite example has always been Starbucks.

How did Howard Shultz scale one coffee shop into 23,768 locations, while in Austin, TX, Sa-Tén Coffee and Eats, for example, only has one store?

They May Want It That Way

While some consultants will be happy to descend upon your business and offer-up expensive analyses of what is holding back your growth, many fail to realize that volume for the sake of volume is not necessarily the answer for everyone. Furthermore, the blind pursuit of growth can actually become counter-productive.

It Versus You

Many people accept the philosophy that your business is your boss; it has certain needs, and therefore it is your responsibility to fulfill them. Whether this conflicts with your kids' baseball or soccer games, your vacation plans, your day off, or your general sanity, some people would say your business should always win.

Why Did You Do It?

Mike Roman often told me that he took the other view. Mike said people create their own business for certain reasons, among them:

- The ability to be your own boss.
- The possibility of unlimited income.
- A place to make things happen.

Mike further emphasized that these things could occur even if your business wasn't number one in sales, events or even profitability.

The Four-Hour Work Week Nonsense

I am not suggesting you don't have to work hard (and smart), and I'm not offering a magic method that would allow you to make lots of money while lying on the beach. Businesses want money, and they're great at asking you for it. You do have the power, however, to tell your business to back off.

Again, Why?

If you started your restaurant or catering business with the goal of becoming the biggest in your city, then your state, and who knows where else, quit reading this and go back to work—you have lots of things to do.

Old-school business people sometimes would say, "if you buy a small business, you've bought yourself a job." They didn't say it derisively though, and this may be where you're at.

You may gross $700,000 per year, have company cars for you and your spouse and have your health insurance paid by your business. Of course you eat for free, and there are a lot of things, like that power washer you bought at Costco, that you can take home and put to good personal use.

If you need to go the the doctor or dentist one afternoon, you don't have to ask anyone if that's OK, and if you want to leave early to see your daughter's game, you can figure out a way to make that happen.

And don't forget one of my top personal reasons for owning your own business— unlimited use of a private dumpster! (I'm not kidding).

It's OK

My point is that just because you own a business doesn't mean you have to do everything possible to max out sales and grow exponentially.

Some people have problems with rapid growth strategies since they require a totally different mindset than a Mom and Pop company. But please do not let anyone tell you that being a small, single-unit company is bad, or not ambitious enough, because it ain't nobody's business but yours, and you do have the power to control it.

THE ACCIDENTAL CATERER

I have to share this story with you all. It comes from my friend Richard Radbil – a veteran of the catering industry and one of Wisconsin's most successful caterers.

Here's the story as told to me by Richard:

My wife and I opened a glorified Chicago-style hot dog stand as our first restaurant. We occupied a 700 square foot hole in the wall, we were all carryout-out and only many months after we opened did we finally added some tables and chairs.

 After we had been in business for about a year, a customer asked if we would cater a party at his house; he and his friends were going to watch a football game, and they thought it would be great if the restaurant came to them.

No Idea

Of course I said yes, and the thought that our restaurant was going to have a day with 30 extra customers that didn't even have to be served on premise was exciting. We knew nothing about catering, and I did the job myself.

I brought a pot to boil the hot dogs, another pot to heat the Italian beef au jus, and all of the appropriate condiments. Luckily, our customers were easily pleased and could have cared less about presentation, so we survived the event.

Here and There

Once in a great while, another customer would ask us to cater a birthday party or a similar small event, and again, we would always say yes. Since these parties were sporadic, we never felt the need to develop systems; this was merely a little side business for some extra cash.

Slow in the Summer

Our restaurant was located in Milwaukee, Wisconsin in the Marquette University area, and the majority of our customers were students. Even though there were summer school sessions, June, July and August could be very slow, as most of our customers would go home for the season.

Wisconsin residents lived for those three months, however, since the warm weather could be fleeting. It seemed that almost every business held a picnic or tailgate party for their employees, and after a customer had asked us to cater one of these events, we decided to actively try and get more, and after a few years, we were catering over one-hundred and fifty of these summer events per year.

Full Time Caterers

After a number of years, for various reasons, we decided to sell our restaurant and become corporate caterers. As I have mentioned before, Mike Roman helped us with menus, but we had very few memorialized systems.

I specifically remember that when our first box lunch order arrived, I spent the morning putting the boxes together. [By the time we sold our catering business, we never had less than 500 boxes ready to go.]

As our business, grew, we realized that the systems were the key. We developed standards for food and paper quantities, had delivery times down to the minute and knew what we could safely prepare the day before. In short, we figured out what we were doing.

It Took a While

This process took us years to figure out. We had many days when things didn't go as smoothly as they should have, and as we sat down and crafted solutions, we swore we would never make the same mistake twice.

The Advantage

Mike Roman was literally the only catering consultant out there when we started.

There was no website—since there was no Internet—and while there may have been some old school catering books we could have looked at, we didn't have time to go to the library and find them.

Today, you have www.TheCorporateCaterer.com

6 TIPS TO BETTER UNDERSTAND DELIVERY CHARGES

Some of us will only fly Southwest Airlines if possible. There's way less hassle involved with changing a flight, and there are no extra charges for checking bags.

Other airlines feast on added charges, but Southwest has found a way to be very profitable without them.

Caterers who charge extra for a piece of cheese on a sandwich or for substituting a brownie for a cookie in a box lunch may be doing more harm than good.

In the drop-off catering business, however, there is one added-charge area where savvy operators make money, and that is with delivery charges.

Customers do understand that it costs money for your company to deliver their food on time. These costs are above and beyond the normal expenses for food, labor, and packaging.

It is reasonable to add a delivery charge for each drop off catering order. As with any extra charge, care has to be taken, so take the following guidelines into consideration as you think about delivery charge theory.

1) First check competitor's delivery charges. You don't want to be the only one who charges $30.00 when everyone else is at $20.00 or below.

2) Consider a flat rate for all deliveries, regardless of distance. Note the success the Post Office has had with flat rate Priority Mail marketing. You can always tack on a surcharge for a true long distance order. *Prix fixe* is the way to go!

3) Alternatively, you could have two or three delivery charge tiers, based on distance.

4) Ensure the customer is notified up front about the delivery charge. No one likes surprises.

5) Check local state taxing regulations to see if you should charge sales tax on the delivery fee.

Some customers don't like paying even a few cents of extra sales tax if it is not mandated by your state.

6) If you pick up some equipment later, don't add another charge for this service. Customers are usually annoyed by this practice.

If you don't already charge a delivery fee, think about the impact that even an extra $10.00 per invoice would have on your gross income. If you have ten orders per day, then that's $100 per day, $500 per week or $25,000 per year. That certainly would be nice to have in your checking account at the end of the year!

Your Own Dog and Pony Show

When I opened my first restaurant I didn't want it to exactly feel like a Mom & Pop place— even though it basically was. This was in the 1970s when restaurant chains were more admired than disdained like they sometimes are today.

Chain restaurants had specially printed paper supplies, fancy logos and custom menu boards behind the counter. Independent restaurants often used generic foam cups, and plastic lettered signs given to them by Coke or Pepsi.

As soon as we opened, I found a place to special print our French fry bags and K-wax with our specially designed logo. I did everything we could to look like I owned more than one restaurant, even though of course I didn't.

As I moved deeper into the catering business, I did the same thing. I found a place in Tennessee to special print the 4 x 4 x 2.5 cake boxes we used for box lunches. I printed our logo and contact info on our napkins, so every buffet was a walking advertisement. I even found a place that would print plastic beer cups. All of this made us look bigger than we were.

Next, we repainted and lettered our trucks. All of our employees wore branded t-shirts and hats, and we even ordered specially sized disposable boxes to transport our box lunches.

Our logo was on everything we sent to clients, and we made sure our email tag lines were up-to-date and slick.

Of course, this cost money, but I'm sure that these actions more than paid for themselves. Any first-time customers were quickly put at ease by the way our food looked, the way our staff looked, and the general way we presented our business to them.

When printed menus were more popular than online versions, we made sure that ours were professionally set up and printed. When everything moved online, we quickly made the transition and had a quality vendor design and develop our site.

While these thoughts may seem obvious, not everyone practices them. There are a lot of excuses that can be employed from "I barely have time to get the food out," to "there's no way I can find the money to do that kind of branding." If you use the excuses as excuses, however, you will soon see your competitors pass you by.

I encourage you to take the time to also learn from people who owned other kinds of businesses. You never know what you can pick up and use for your own business. Always keep innovating!

THE MENU – WHERE TO START?

A friend of mine told me about his start in the food service business. Here is a short story.

"Michael here's how it all began. I started in the food business by opening a restaurant. Mine was a glorified Chicago-style hot dog stand named Wales on Wells located in the Marquette University area in Milwaukee, WI.

We rented a 700 square foot space on Wells Street and since my father-in-law's last name was Wales and he provided the initial loan, you can see how the restaurant's name was born.

My wife and I never even considered catering until a customer asked if we could come to his house and bring food while he and his friends watched the Packer's game.

That somehow worked, and eventually, customers asked us to cater picnics and Milwaukee Brewer tailgate parties. Since most of our Marquette clientele left for the summer, outdoor catering was a natural fit for us as it filled in a big revenue gap. We jumped on this opportunity, and soon we were catering over 150 outdoor events each summer!

Since we sold hamburgers, brats, hot dogs and similar items, converting these to a catering menu was easy. If you have a restaurant and want to become a drop-off caterer, it is not difficult to take the things you already serve and morph them into a drop-off catering menu."

His story got me thinking about menus and how the creation of your first can be a daunting task if you aren't familiar with catering.

So let's take an in-depth look:

First, let's consider the meals you need to have menus for. Most corporate caterers do the bulk of their business at lunch. The second most popular meal is breakfast, and while many caterers do a substantial number of dinner-type events, these are usually third on the list. Of course, clients may call you for many other types of deliveries such as afternoon snacks and even cocktail parties, but let's deal with these later. Today, we'll start to consider what you need to present a basic breakfast menu.

Most dropped-off breakfasts can be categorized as hot or cold, and when you are just beginning, you do not need a fancy or extensive menu. As you become comfortable with menu items and you see what your customers like and/or request, you can add to your offerings.

The most common breakfast ordered is the Continental Breakfast. While there are obviously many variations, a good place to start is here:

Catering Cafe's Continental Breakfast:

- Bagels
- Danish
- Scones
- Donuts
- Fresh Fruit
- Assorted Juices
- Coffee/Decaf

Some caterers even like to keep it simpler by putting the Danish, donuts and scones into one area called sweets. You may have other menu items like cinnamon rolls, for example. Regardless, I'm sure you understand the concept.

Another description that allows you more

flexibility based on your inventory is a rotating assortment of fresh baked goods.

You do need to include plates, napkins, flatware, cups, etc.; some caterers charge for these and others do not. As we progress, we will discuss the advantages and disadvantages of different pricing philosophies.

Building menus are not that difficult if you start simply and add, as you get deeper into drop-off catering. All you need to do is just give it a try and get started! Action leads to results.

10 POINT PLAN TO MANAGE YOUR PAPERWORK

The key to successfully dealing with your paperwork is to keep up with it. Granted, this is easier said than done. If you are starting with one big mess, the first thing to do is sift through it and decide what to keep and what to throw away.

1) Purge

Throw away, shred, and recycle all junk mail, catalogs, and out-of-date information. Be aggressive. When in doubt, throw it out.

2) Open all mail

Trash all advertising inserts. If you pay your bills online, discard all payment envelopes. Shred loan offers and checks from credit card companies immediately. Don't even look at them.

3) Sort in Piles (or Storage bins if necessary)

Examples: Bills / Bank Statements / Correspondence

4) One-by-one take immediate action

Starting with one pile, resolve what to do with every single piece of paper in front of you. Do not postpone these decisions.

5) Do it

Chances are you will either have to Pay it, File it, Record it, Respond to it, Sign it or Scan it. Do not create a new pile for any of it.

6) Implement this system – daily

Have an "IN BOX" on your desk for new arrivals.

7) Create a To-Shred box.

Appropriate paperwork should be added daily.

8) Organize your passwords and usernames

Use a software program such as One Password and /or keep a hard copy safely filed.

9) Vendor List

Keep ALL of your vendors listed by the name of the company. Include the phone number, contact person, account number, ordering information. Add to it as needed and post it so that it is accessible to your staff.

10) Straighten up at the end of the day.

This should only take few minutes. Get rid of what you can and tidy up what is left. Once a week, wipe down your desk, monitors, and keyboards.

Keep in mind, walking into an organized office every day makes a difference for you and your employees!

5 REASONS WHY RESTAURANT OWNERS AVOID CATERING?

Despite the fact that adding catering services can be highly lucrative, many restaurant owners avoid offering catering services. Following are five reasons why some restaurant owners avoid offering catering services.

1. No Time

Many business owners are too busy managing day-to-day operations, putting out fires, and trying to make ends-meet. They simple do not believe they have time to plan and launch a catering operation.

2. Financial Uncertainty

If an owner is struggling to make payroll and

pay vendors, they may not be able to leverage the necessary resources.

3. Burnout

Some owners are simple burnt. They have worked for years in the food industry, and now they just go through the motions.

The passion is gone. They are not interested in expanding operations or assuming more responsibilities.

4. Lack of Knowledge

It is difficult to imagine taking on something if you have little or no knowledge about it. Although restaurants and catering are both parts of the food industry, they are numerous differences.

Managing a successful and profitable restaurant catering operation requires gathering and learning new information. Ideally, the restaurant owner who is interested in offering catering services should turn and seek insights and strategies from someone who has managed a successful and profitable restaurant catering operation.

5. Fear

Some restaurant owners are simply afraid to offer catering services. Let's face it; fear plays a role. Regardless if a restaurant owner chooses to offer catering or not, there is always an element of fear that needs to be overcome.

Any new business venture tends to come with some risk. The question is: Does the person embrace the challenge or give into the fear.

With all of these reasons in mind, remember, it's never too late to start catering. If you've been fearful of catering for some of the reasons above, there are always ways to work around the issues and start earning more business by catering! Taking action is the key. Build a plan, get started and grow your business through catering.

~A Baker's Dozen~

13 Answers to 13 Frequently Asked ?'s

As a catering coach/consultant, I'm asked lots of questions. In fact, I've complied a list of "101 Answers to 101 Frequently Asked Questions about Your Catering Business. Here's a taste.

#1 (Q) "We've built our reputation as a full-service caterer. We want to break into the corporate drop-off market. While our corporate business starting to grow, we are anxious for it to grow faster. Any suggestions?

(A) You're expanding your brand, which means you want to shift consumer perception. Create a separate, corporate drop-off menu and link on your website. Promote this new division of your business through social media and e-mail marketing.

Offer complimentary Tastings to businesses in you area that order catering regularly. Host an open house. Invite the people who order catering to sample your corporate menu.

Have your staff present to answer questions and engage your prospects. Remember, you are starting a new business within your business. It will take commitment, persistence and patience.

* * * * *

#2 (Q) " Should I give my corporate drop-off division a separate name?"

(A) There is no right or wrong answer. Some clients add, "Express" or "Delivery" or "Corporate Catering" after the name. (Example: Emma's Catering: Express). Others will reference their "Corporate Catering Division." If you decide on a separate name, consider a separate phone number as well.

*   *   *   *   *

#3 (Q) "Can you suggest a creative, affordable marketing idea?"

(A) Put your company name/logo and phone number/website on the roof of your delivery vehicle(s) as well as the sides. Anyone looking through their office window will see your company information.

*   *   *   *   *

#4 (Q) "When is an order big enough that two (or more) people are required for delivery and set- up?"

(A) It depends. You could have an order for 200 people, but if it's only coffee and desserts, one person should be able to handle it. Lunch for 200 people is a different story.

Considerations include:

 * How much set-up time your delivery person has available?

 * Are you delivering hot food or box lunches?

 * Are cans/bottles of drinks included? (It adds time to set-up).

 * What is the "ease of delivery factor" to the specific company?

With larger orders, I suggest being safe rather than sorry. (I've travelled the Sorry Road, it's not fun). If you're on the fence, send a second person.

Sometimes we have two people go together and get everything unloaded and into the company.

One stays and sets-up, while the other makes

other drop-offs in the area - and then circles back to pick-up their partner, or helps finish setting-up, if necessary.

* * * * *

#5 (Q) "Do you always set-up the order? Do you ever just drop it off at reception?"

(A) We always offer to set-up. For some clients, it's an important component of our service. I'm constantly reminding our delivery representatives, "You're the faces of this business. Your job is to make each customer feel as if they are the most important customer of your day.

* * * * *

#6 (Q) "When someone without a corporate account wants to place their first order, and asks to be billed, will you do that?"

(A) No. We politely explain the first order is required to go on a credit card. (We retain the information). Then, we email them a link to the Account Application Form on our website. We tell once the form is completed, we can bill them for all future orders.

*   *   *   *   *

#7 (Q) "How do you handle an end-of-the day call from a customer requesting a labor-intensive hot meal, such as lasagna for 40 people for the next day? Especially when the kitchen crew is gone for the day?"

(A) When the kitchen is producing lasagnas, always make extra and freeze them. The person who takes the order can pull them from the freezer so they will thaw by the next day. (Note: Do this with other popular, freezable entrees).

*   *   *   *   *

#8 (Q) "How do I handle requests for same day orders?"

(A) Embrace them. As your business grows, calls for same-day orders will increase. With your chef, establish which production-friendly, same-day menu items you can offer. If you are booked solid for noon deliveries, tell your customer you can deliver by 12:30. If you are serious about becoming a player in your corporate catering market, you must be able to accommodate same days order to the best of your capabilities.

* * * * *

#9 (Q) " How much should I charge for delivery?"

(A) Check out what your competitors are charging for delivery and stay within that range. If you're providing quality, on-time delivery, err on the higher side of the range. Delivery / service charges are bottom line revenue that adds up quickly.

* * * * *

#10 (Q) "We have had the same catering menu for years. Should we change it up periodically?

(A) Absolutely yes. Especially when you have created repeat business. This process does not have to be as time consuming as you may think. When I review a coaching / consulting clients menu, it often has more entrees, sandwiches, sides and salads than are necessary.

A big menu can be overwhelming for some potential customers. For example, if you have ten chicken entrees, remove four. In six months, put them back on the menu and remove four others. Do the same for sandwiches sides and salads. Another tip is to feature one or two as a "Seasonal Specials" and rotate those four times a year. This works – trust me.

*　　*　　*　　*　　*

#11 (Q) "When setting up hot food in chafers, sometimes we're running around a customer's office looking for a kitchen or bathroom for water. Making multiple trips back and forth draws some inquiring looks and feels unprofessional. Any thoughts?

(A) Bring hot water with you. Fill air pots or

Cambros from the hot water dispenser on your coffee machine.

*   *   *   *   *

#12 (Q) "We are easily able to track sales for our three divisions: 1) Corporate drop-off catering, 2) Full-service catering, and 3) Restaurant/Café. Separating expenses has been much more difficult. How do you suggest allocating expenses to our different divisions?

(A) This is challenging. We have tried different methodologies and concluded it will never be perfect. Some expenses such as labor, paper products, and china rentals are easier to categorize.

Food costs are trickier. When a $400 produce order comes in and three different departments are grabbing from it, determining how to allocate the costs can make your head spin.

Create a system that is as accurate as possible, within reason. At minimum, always be aware of the financial heath of your operation as a whole.

*   *   *   *   *

#13 (Q) "I can't afford a sales person and have no one to make cold calls. How do I get lists of businesses in my area that order catering?"

(A) Call The Corporate Caterer at 781-641-3303 and ask about The Leads Program. You give them the zip codes where you want to go after new corporate catering business and they do all the cold calling for you. This will save you an enormous amount of time.

Made in the USA
Middletown, DE
17 March 2017